HERTFORDSHIRE

Above Hertfordshire's future, present and past.
A bridesmaid after a wedding at
Old Welwyn church.

Following page The county's landscape.
Looking towards Sandon.

HERTFORDSHIRE

A PORTRAIT IN COLOUR

PHOTOGRAPHS BY JOHN HODDER
TEXT BY JOHN LUCAS

THE DOVECOTE PRESS

The half-timbered five hundred year-old Patchetts,
Hilfield Lane, Aldenham.

First published in 1993 by The Dovecote Press Ltd
Stanbridge, Wimborne, Dorset BH21 4JD

ISBN 1 874336 18 0

Photographs © John Hodder 1993
Text © John Lucas 1993

Designed by Humphrey Stone

Photoset in Sabon by The Typesetting Bureau, Wimborne, Dorset
Origination by Chroma Graphics (Overseas) Pte Ld, Singapore
Printed and bound by Kim Hup Lee Printing Co Pte Ltd, Singapore

British Library Cataloguing-in-Publication Data
A catalogue record of this book is
available from the British Library

CONTENTS

NEW TOWNS AND OLD 9

BISHOP'S STORTFORD AND
THE RURAL EAST 29

THE CHILTERNS AND THE WEST 59

ST ALBANS AND HATFIELD 73

HERTFORD AND THE LEA VALLEY 91

WATFORD AND THE SOUTH 107

The Photographs 126

Acknowledgements 126

Index 127

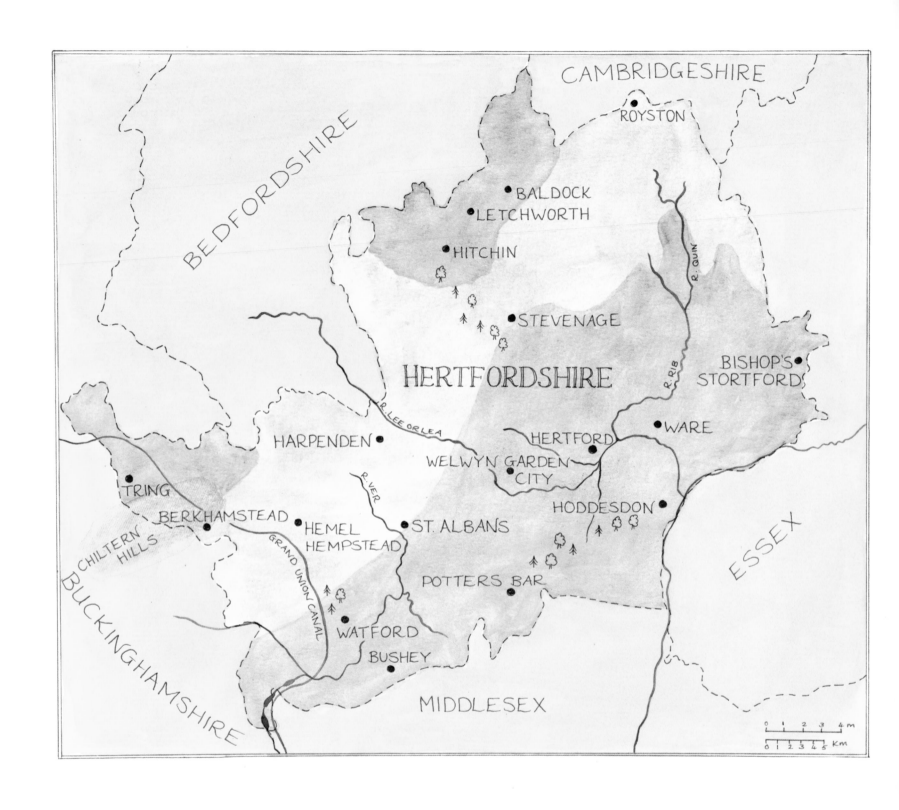

HERTFORDSHIRE

In *Howards End*, E.M. Forster, who spent part of his life in Stevenage, wrote that Hertfordshire's 'delicate structure particularly needs the attentive eye. Hertfordshire is England at its quietest, with little emphasis of river and hill; it is England meditative'.

Forster was writing in 1910 – a world away. But what better medium for that attentive eye than a camera in the hands of a discerning photographer? In the following pages, John Hodder's pictures breathe abundant life into the traditional view of the county.

Hertfordshire is home to a million of us; it is among the smallest and most densely populated of England's counties. Yet because of its proximity to London and the seats of power, the county's history has often marched hand-in-hand with England's own.

There is plenty of evidence of settlers from the Stone and Bronze Ages. Later the Belgae came out from Europe's mainland, crossing the Channel and moving up the Rivers Thames and Lea to central Hertfordshire. Then there were the Roman invasions and the establishment of the first town in Hertfordshire at Verulamium – now St Albans – followed by clashes with Boudicca, warrior queen of the Iceni.

History then ranged widely. Alban, a Roman soldier, became the first Christian martyr, on the hill above Verulamium. The throne of England was surrendered to William the Conqueror at Berkhamsted. There was the accession of the young princess, Elizabeth, at Hatfield as the queen under whom England flourished as never before. The Gunpowder Plot was exposed at Furneux Pelham. An assassination attempt on Charles II's life was planned near Hoddesdon. Much later, three Prime Ministers in Victoria's reign lived in the county.

The Victorian period brought huge changes to Hertfordshire. Come the Industrial Revolution and railway fever, and out puffed trains from London, in their smoky wake bringing more people, demanding more houses and forming bigger towns. Around Forster's time, the population of Stevenage was a mere 5,000; today it is 75,000. Fortunately there were benevolent influences equal to the task of softening the effects of this population explosion, notably Ebenezer Howard, that admirable visionary and creator of our garden cities, among which Letchworth and Welwyn Garden City stand as an abiding tribute and memorial.

After the Second World War came the New Towns, and the need to come to terms with another massive population overspill from London. One has now only to draw a line from north to south just east of the A1 to realise the great disparity in population between the west of the county and the east, with its single sizeable town, Bishop's Stortford. It is almost as if the east is the back garden and kitchen garden of the more heavily populated and industrial west, led by Watford. Fortunately, the original villages and towns which have served as the nuclei of the new, have in general had their identities preserved.

Lacking roots in Hertfordshire, as our photographer John Hodder admits, he has served in the role of spectator. But he has also seen the county with a fresh eye, thus perhaps tempering with realism my romantic view as a Hertfordshire resident. My necessarily more subjective role has been a heartwarming experience, and one which has enabled me to recapture and re-savour days long since vanished.

For in my half-remembered youth in the 1930s, my father would drive us from our home in North London into the bracing Hertfordshire air at Crews Hill, Cuffley, Bayford or Little Berkhamsted, armed with the excellent books of walks then produced by London Transport. We would stroll the paths, lanes and woodlands, watch village cricket the while, pause for refreshment at the teashops that then abounded, and often lose our sense of time and find ourselves walking back to the car at dusk accompanied now by the harvest moon.

To me, Hertfordshire is what that great lover of the county, Charles Lamb, described in his essays as 'hearty, homely, loving Hertfordshire', which thankfully it often still is. Those winding lanes, with their hedges and ditches, the tilting meadows of cows and sheep and acres of corn, the fine village churches, grand houses and little thatched cottages... all are welded in my mind into a single evocation of Hertfordshire's delights.

Is my hindsight over-tinted with romance? Possibly so. Certainly the ambience of those lanes has changed. The occasional car that puttered along in the Thirties and Forties is likelier now to be moving at such a speed that the hapless walker is forced to retreat on to the field paths in sheer self-defence.

Before the Second World War, my father traced one branch of our family to eighteenth-century Hertfordshire. It is a county that proliferates with those bearing my name. So I should like to dedicate my contribution to this book to them, and to those of our forebears who also settled happily within its borders.

JOHN LUCAS
Potters Bar

NEW TOWNS AND OLD

NEW TOWNS AND OLD

The outward appearance of Hertfordshire between Letchworth in the north and south to Welwyn has changed out of all recognition during the course of this century. Geographically fourteen miles apart, the two towns are united in Ebenezer Howard's vision of the Garden City. In about 1900, Howard articulated widely felt anxieties about the then poor living conditions of working people in Britain. In Hertfordshire he was able to translate his revolutionary ideas into practice, by providing harmonious living and working environments.

There has been even greater change between the two towns comprising Stevenage – once just a village on the old Great North Road but now, as first in a rash of post-war New Towns, grown into the third largest town in Hertfordshire after Watford and Hemel Hempstead.

Old Stevenage has been left alone and thrives nearby. Hitchin, on the other hand, is neither garden city nor new town. Despite the traffic that is the curse of all old market towns, its centre, comfortably accompanied by streets containing period buildings, is still a delight to the eye, and the venerable St Mary's church remains a rich and enduring jewel in its crown.

South of Hitchin, down towards Wheathampstead, it is still possible to lose oneself in a glorious tangle of lanes, fields and woods. It was in this part of the county that that waggish sage George Bernard Shaw lived for forty-four years in his adopted village of Ayot St Lawrence. In his *Rhyming Picture Guide*, fittingly his last work, Shaw expressed a life's contentment there.

> This is my dell, and this my dwelling.
> Their charm so far beyond my telling,
> That though in Ireland is my birthplace,
> This house shall be my final earthplace.

'Their charm so far beyond my telling. . .' Few people, I suspect, living and strolling in this part of the county would not echo such words.

Previous page The fountains in Parkway, Welwyn Garden City.

Right A cyclist amid cow parsley and corn in early summer near King's Walden.

Ayot St Lawrence, a village near Wheathampstead, has two churches – one old and partly demolished by Sir Lyonel Lyde because it spoilt his view from Ayot House. The other is 'new'. In 1778 he built this classical-style church to replace the old one and improve his view. There are two pavilions, one either side of the church, built thus because Sir Lyonel's marriage had not been a success and he was determined that the church that had united him and his wife should not do so in death. In one pavilion lie the remains of Sir Lyonel, in the other those of Lady Lyde. The church, which is in regular use, is visible from the village and can be reached by a footpath. The playwright and sage George Bernard Shaw lived at nearby Shaw's Corner for forty-four years, until his death in 1950. Owned by the National Trust, Shaw's Corner is open to the public, and the great man's belongings, including his working desk, have been left as they were in his lifetime.

Above A salutary warning to hotel visitors and passers-by is this sign in Bucklersbury, Hitchin, outside the sixteenth-century Red Hart Hotel. The last public hanging is believed to have taken place in the yard there.

Right Hitchin has many fine old buildings, among them these timber-fronted houses in Tilehouse Street, a short walk from the town centre.

Left A train crossing the lofty Digswell viaduct en route for Kings Cross. The 40-arch railway viaduct was designed by Lewis Cubitt and built by Thomas Brassey in 1850 to span the valley of the River Mimram, and is one of the finest examples of industrial architecture in the county. Queen Victoria, however, was not impressed, and refused to travel across it. According to local lore, she had her train stop at the start of the viaduct, and insisted on being conveyed across the valley by coach.

Hitchin's pride, the splendid medieval church of St Mary near the town centre. Its ancestor was a Benedictine house built by King Offa to mark his victory in battle in AD 758. In the middle ages, the wool from the sheep that grazed the nearby hillsides made the town prosperous, as did the wheat and barley grown to its north for the London breweries. Much of this wealth is represented in the size and rich architecture of St Mary's – which no other Hertfordshire church can rival.

Right The impressive medieval vaulting in the two-storey porch of St Mary's, Hitchin, part of which dates from the twelfth century. A sundial dated 1660 – the year of the Restoration of the Monarchy – is clearly visible on the tower.

The glorious Palladian-style bridge over the River Lea, with Brocket Hall, near Wheathampstead, in the background. Two nineteenth-century Prime Ministers, Lord Melbourne and Lord Palmerston, died at the Hall, which was also the setting of a scandal involving Melbourne's beautiful wife, the notorious Lady Caroline Lamb. Lady Caroline had become infatuated with the poet Lord Byron, but became mentally deranged after a chance encounter with the cortege taking Byron's corpse back to Nottinghamshire for burial following his death in Greece in 1824, and she died four years later. Lord Melbourne acted as guide and mentor to the young Queen Victoria after she came to the throne in 1837, and he died at Brocket Hall in 1848. Palmerston died there in 1865. Brocket Hall remains in the hands of the Brocket family, and is now a residential conference centre.

Rolling pastureland and woods near King's Walden, west of Stevenage. Not far away is the eighteenth-century home of the Bowes Lyon family for the last 250 years, St Paul's Walden Bury. Queen Elizabeth the Queen Mother, who was born in London, was baptised in St Paul's Walden church, and spent much of her childhood at the Bury. The gardens are occasionally open to visitors.

Turrets, cupolas, gargoyles and dragons lend a slightly bizarre appearance to the upper facade of Knebworth House. When Sir Edward Bulwer-Lytton (1803-1873) inherited the house in 1843 he added these adornments in an attempt to turn it into a Gothic palace. The main body of the building is much older – dating back to around 1500. Bulwer-Lytton is now largely unread, but his epic historical novels were Victorian bestsellers. Among the most famous was *The Last Days of Pompeii* – hence perhaps the classical bust in the smaller photograph. Today, the House, gardens and park are a popular attraction, as is the Raj Collection, a permanent exhibition recalling the great days of the British Empire and the role of Sir Robert Bulwer (1831-1891), Viceroy of India, later the 1st Earl of Lytton. It was Sir Robert who organised the Delhi Durbar of 1877 at which Queen Victoria was proclaimed Empress of India. Knebworth is owned today by Cameron Cobbold, the 2nd Baron.

Right A lone stag crossing a ride in Knebworth Park.

To Letchworth – or rather, to its designer, Sir Ebenezer Howard (1850-1928) – goes the credit for the first garden city in Britain, developed in 1903. The aerial view of the Kennedy Gardens (formerly the Rose Gardens), and the tree-lined streets radiating off them, clearly illustrate Howard's intention to create green spaces in the heart of the city centre, provide every house with a garden and offer easy access to the surrounding countryside. Howard's belief in the idea of the garden city sprang out of a general dissatisfaction with the poor quality of workers' living conditions in Britain. He was totally disinterested in money, but such was his enthusiasm he was able to convince town-planners and financiers that his ideas made sense. The two other photographs are of the Old Grammar School, built in 1912, and some of the original early twentieth-century houses.

One of many industries that sprang up in Letchworth Garden City between the wars was Irvin Great Britain, makers of the first emergency parachutes for the Royal Air Force. Parachutes are seen here in the hanging bay at the Icknield Way factory, established in 1926. Irvin's founder was Leslie Leroy Irvin, an American circus performer and stunt man who came to Britain and set up business after impressing the Government with his life-saving freefall parachute. Since then, Irvin-designed parachutes have saved more than 100,000 lives throughout the world.

Tower blocks at Bedwell in Stevenage, a rural town whose expansion was foreshadowed before the Second World War and is now the county's third largest with a population of 75,000 (Watford has 84,000, Hemel Hempstead 79,000). Stevenage's role as the first of the new towns intended to syphon off some of Greater London's fast-expanding population began in 1946, and the first of the planned 'neighbourhoods' – Stevenage has at least 20 shopping centres – was begun in 1949. The first new factories followed shortly afterwards, and the since much-imitated but then revolutionary concept of creating a pedestrian town centre was initiated in 1958.

Left Feeding the ducks in Fairlands Valley Park, Stevenage's main open space.

Below Old Stevenage High Street – busy, but still a contrast to the bustle of its still expanding new-town neighbour. Old Stevenage once stood on the Great North Road, in the old days infested with highwaymen. Dick Turpin (1705-1739) arranged a farewell meeting with his wife at the Roebuck Inn, at the southern end of the town, before fleeing to Yorkshire: he galloped off when he spotted a constable.

Right Schoolchildren make their way towards the miniature railway in the grounds of Knebworth House, with Stevenage visible through the background haze.

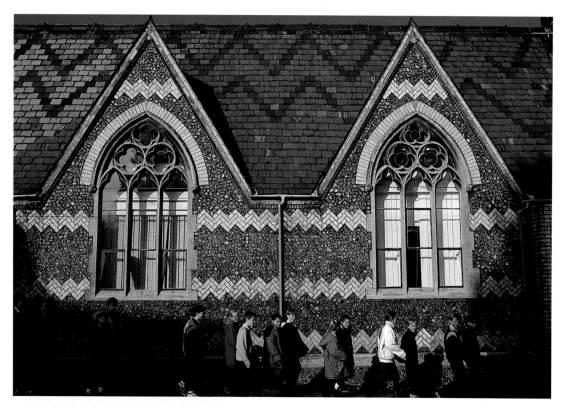

Left Few Victorian village schools were as attractive as this one, which stands near St Helen's Church in Wheathampstead, and boasts flint and brick facing, horizontal zigzag stripes and a green and grey tiled roof. Despite the presence of the children, it is now used as offices.

Below Looking past St Mary's church door towards the timbered Wellington Inn and Old Welwyn High Street. The inn's guests have included Samuel Pepys, Dr Johnson and David Garrick. Another visitor to Welwyn was the painter Vincent van Gogh, and a plaque on a house in nearby Church Street notes that he would walk all the way from London to visit his sister, who lived in Old Welwyn in 1873.

Poplars framing the decorative gardens in Howardsgate, Welwyn Garden City. Welwyn was the second garden city founded by Ebenezer Howard, and was laid out in 1920 on an agricultural estate that Howard had bought with the help of friends at an auction in the previous year. Howard died at his house in Welwyn in 1928 and is commemorated by the bas-relief shown in the foregound. The inscription reads: 'His vision and practical idealism profoundly affected town planning throughout the world'.

A solitary oak amid ploughed fields in the open rolling landscape typical of the north-western corner of the county.

The lychgate of All Saints' Church, Willian, near Letchworth. The carved tablet above the gate commemorates the nine men of the village who gave their lives in the First World War. The church is mainly fifteenth century, though a door in the chancel dates back to the twelfth. There is an interesting roadside memorial beside Wymondley Road, near Willian, to two Royal Flying Corps officers, who died in 1912 in one of the earliest air crashes.

BISHOP'S STORTFORD AND THE RURAL EAST

BISHOP'S STORTFORD AND THE RURAL EAST

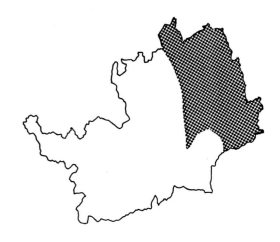

Last century's railway revolution, which drew people out into Hertfordshire, left much of the eastern area untouched: farming continued as it had always done. But the nature of farming has changed too, bringing more mechanisation, fewer workers – and a crop of problems, not least of which is 'set aside', generated by the European Community. As a result, many Londoners, encouraged by lower property prices, have over the years moved out from the city and its suburbs and settled in the villages north-west of Bishop's Stortford, commuting to London by train, or by car down the motorways.

East Hertfordshire's attractions are undeniable. From the eastern tip of the Chilterns in the north down to Sawbridgeworth in the south, there is rolling pasture and cornlands. Timbered whitewashed cottages abound – at the Hadhams, for example – many with the decorative plasterwork that is a valued adornment all along the Hertfordshire border and east into Essex.

Previous page The rich arable corn country near Benington.

Looking past the village hall towards the green and wellhouse at Ardeley, north-east of Stevenage. The church opposite is medieval, and the vicarage seventeenth century, but the green and surrounding thatched houses are younger than they seem. Planned jointly by the vicar, Dr H. V. S. Eck, and John Howard Carter, owner of Ardeley Bury, all were built and laid out during and after the First World War. This part of Hertfordshire is famous for an historic case of alleged witchcraft. A mile or so to the south-west of the village is Walkern, home of Jane Wenham, the last witch to be condemned to death. At her trial in 1711, a jury found her guilty and the judge passed sentence. But Jane had apparently been intimidated into confessing, and so was reprieved, pardoned by Queen Anne and freed. The case was important because no 'witch' has ever received the death sentence again. Ardeley is the birthplace in 1632 of Sir Henry Chauncy, the first Hertfordshire historian, whose monumental work was published in 1700.

Ashwell church, in one of the county's northernmost, and most interesting, villages. A Latin inscription on the north interior wall of the church tower, possibly carved by a monk after the Black Death, bewails the misery of the plague, which struck the village in 1349. There is also a carved drawing of what is thought to be the original pre-Wren version of St Paul's Cathedral. Ashwell acquired its name from the springs in the village centre, from which more than a million gallons of fresh spring water a day eventually empty into the Wash, sixty-five miles away.

Peaceful as the eastern county may be, however, history has not ignored it. But in some places the tide of history has receded, leaving its villages happily cast up in a quiet backwater. Under the Roman occupation, for example, Braughing was a settlement, second only in importance to St Albans, and lay at the hub of several important roads to other Roman centres. Buntingford stood on Ermine Street, the Romans' main route from the Wash to Salisbury Plain.

History is measured in aeons here. Neolithic barrows are to be seen near Royston. At Ashwell, slightly west, a poignant contemporary inscription in the church speaks to us across six hundred years of the agonies of the Black Death. At Thorley, Dick Whittington held lands. In Furneux Pelham lay the key to the foiling of the Gunpowder Plot. The empire builder Cecil Rhodes was a native of Bishop's Stortford. At Standon Green End a balloonist landed after risking his life making the first flight over England.

More recently, Perry Green was for many years the home of the great sculptor Henry Moore, some of whose work can still be seen there in its natural setting.

Happily, those little eastern villages still evoke the agricultural character of the landscape in which they sit. Commuters may today share the lanes with tractors, but the open corn-lands, with their panoramic views and intimate little chalk streams, still remain the most rural part of the county.

A distant view of Baldock. The town is thought to owe its name to a group of Knights Templar who settled in the area following their defeat by the Saracens in the Crusades at a place called Baldach. It is Hertfordshire's most northerly town, and grew up on the success of its malting and brewing trades. Like Old Stevenage, it lay on the original Great North Road, and in coaching days it was the first main stopping point after leaving London.

Right Hitchin Street, Baldock, where there were once at least six inns in the town's coaching hey-day.

The octagonal lantern and spire (known as a 'Hertfordshire spike') on Baldock's early fourteenth-century St Mary's church, seen here behind eighteenth-century houses in the High Street. There is much of interest inside the church, and its silver includes the Byrd chalice, so-called because a rector, Josiah Byrd, gave Charles I a drink from it on his way through Baldock to London after his arrest. In the churchyard lies another notable cleric, the Rev. John Smith, who spent three years deciphering Samuel Pepys's diaries from his own shorthand into longhand.

An unusual and striking view of the two great
dishes that are familiar landmarks to travellers
along the Royston Road (A505) about two miles
east of Baldock. They belong to the International
Satellite Monitoring Station, which records
emissions from satellites. The Station also receives
reports of radio interference.

Bringing in the harvest near Clothall, a village south-east of Baldock.

Left This rare 'gallows' sign, spanning a road and depicting a hunting scene, gives a rural flavour to the Fox and Hounds inn at Barley, near Royston. The inn dates from the fifteenth century, and was originally known as the Waggon & Horses. When an inn in Barley called the Fox and Hounds was burned down in 1950, the Waggon & Horses acquired both the sign – and its name.

Below left Cottages of tile, timber and plaster line the green at Benington.

Benington Lordship, or manor, is a Georgian house standing on the site of a Norman castle, the ruins of which are still visible. The stone building next to the house is a Norman-style gatehouse, which although imposing is only a folly, built in 1832. But the Lordship can reach genuinely into history, for it was once the seat of the Saxon kings of Mercia, where in 850 a council was held to discuss the disastrous news that the Vikings had captured Canterbury and London.

Contrasting architectural styles line the steep High Street of Bishop's Stortford, Hertfordshire's easternmost town, below St Michael's Church. The father of the great empire builder, and Stortford's most famous son, Cecil Rhodes, was vicar of St Michael's. Rhodes himself went to the local Grammar School and the room where he was born in 1853 is in what is now the Rhodes Memorial Museum and Commonwealth Centre, in South Street, and is furnished as it was then. Rhodes died in 1902 and is buried in the Matopo Hills in Zimbabwe. About a mile from the town, at Thorley, is a manor once held by Richard Whittington, three times Lord Mayor of London, whose story has passed into legend.

Braughing, a village north-west of Bishop's Stortford, was of some importance as a Roman settlement, from which roads radiated to the Roman towns of what are now London, St Albans, Colchester, Cambridge and Godmanchester. It has since acquired a fifteenth-century church, and at least seven reported ghosts – of the Grey Lady, five monks and a friar.

A pleasant jumble of ancient shop fronts and houses in Buntingford High Street, now happily spared the thunder of heavy lorries by the bypass. Buntingford, a small town of 5,000 people, stands on what was Ermine Street, constructed by the Romans to connect London and York, and which now forms a stretch of the A10 between London and Cambridge.

Furneux Pelham Hall, this fine sixteenth-century brick manor house was once the home of Lord Mounteagle, the man who exposed the Gunpowder Plot. Mounteagle, a Catholic peer who sat in the House of Lords, was sent a letter in 1605 which began: 'Retire yourself into the country for. . . they shall receive a terrible blow this Parliament and yet they shall not see who hurts them'. His suspicions aroused, Mounteagle passed the letter to the Privy Council, and the plotters were caught.

Red deer on Pelham Venison's farm at Furneux.

Spraying the potato crop at Great Hormead, east of Buntingford.

A field near Little Hormead of bright yellow oilseed rape – a delight to the eye (if not to the hayfever sufferer's nose) and to the farmer's pocket. Rape yields oil for margarine and cooking oil; what is left makes a useful animal feed. The EC is a net importer of oilseed rape; which is why it encourages farmers to grow it.

A brilliant splash of crimson from a field of poppies near Kelshall, just south-west of Royston – no pleasure to a farmer, perhaps, to whom they are weeds, but a joy to countryside strollers.

The other photograph is of the much rarer Easter anemone, or pasque flower (Anemone pulsatilla), a purple, hair-covered flower blooming in April, which happily thrives alongside cowslips in the chalky grassland on Therfield Heath.

The impressive angel roof of St Mary's, Furneux Pelham. Another feature will have been passed on the way in: the brusque injunction on the external tower wall, 'Time Flies. Mind Your Business'. In the south chapel there are fine stained-glass windows installed in memory of the Calvert family by William Morris and Sir Edward Burne-Jones.

Looking north-east across farm buildings towards Royston from Therfield Heath, and *(below)* a view of pastureland south of the town.

Stable lads exercising racehorses in the early morning mist on Therfield Heath – a favourite hunting ground of James I.

A lone golfer on Royston golf course, another feature of the heath.

A pleasing pattern created by a winter dusting of snow on ploughland near Therfield. There are several burial mounds on Therfield Heath, including a long barrow 125 feet long and ten Bronze Age round barrows, one of which contained nine human skeletons.

Following pages Open farmland on the northern edge of the Chilterns looking towards Kelshall.

A timbered whitewashed cottage in Much
Hadham, and pleasantly typical of the architecture
in the eastern part of the county.

Sheep graze beside a work by Henry Moore on the estate at Perry Green where the sculptor lived and worked for many years. Moore liked his works to be displayed in natural surroundings, but his pieces also make worthy adornments in the new towns – as for example at Stevenage. Since Moore's death in 1986, Dane Tree House at Perry Green has been the headquarters of the Henry Moore Foundation, established by him in 1977 to sponsor art projects and make grants to deserving young sculptors.

The appearance of All Saints Church, Sandon, near Baldock, is made strange by the buttresses supporting the tower. Because of suspected shrinking in the clay subsoil, the tower of the mainly fourteenth-century church was found to be tilting to the west, with the result that these rather ungainly brick supports were added in the eighteenth century – the date 1763 is inscribed on the brickwork. Sandon, which prides itself on maintaining its medieval character, has in recent times been isolated by impassable roads in bad weather.

Looking into Knight Street, Sawbridgeworth, an attractive town to the east of the county near the Essex border. Unusually, the town has developed within a square of streets rather than with a single conventional High Street. Sawbridgeworth was granted a charter for a market and fair in 1306, which now only survives as a small funfair.

The tower of the church of St Andrew and St Mary, with its stair turret, peeps above the trees across fields at Watton-at-Stone. The church figured in the Civil War, when Parliamentary troops used it to house Royalist prisoners.

Standon village green, with the attractive brick and timber Endowed School building – now dwellings – in the background. On the green itself is one of several boulders of a rock called puddingstone, which is found largely in Hertfordshire. Until 1904 this piece formed part of the wall of the churchyard. Puddingstone, which was often used in church buildings, is a sixty million-year-old conglomerate of a natural 'cement' and coloured pebbles, and resembles concrete. The Romans used it for whetstones, and because it can be highly polished it is sometimes used to make jewellery. Standon village church, St Mary's, is unique in that its tower stands quite detached from the main building, which sits on a slope. The oak tree in this picture was planted in 1911 to commemorate the coronation of King George V.

The stone within these railings, in a meadow at Standon Green End, north of Ware, marks a historic event: a landing by the Italian aeronaut Vincenzo Lunardi, who in 1784 was the first man to make a balloon flight over England. A metal hinged flap on the obelisk reveals an inscription about the flight. His journey was certainly courageous: the Montgolfier brothers in France had staged the first balloon flight of all time only the previous year. Lunardi had taken off from the Artillery Ground at Finsbury Square, London and briefly touched down at Welham Green, near Hatfield, where a hostile reception from local people forced him to take off again. Lunardi's epic flight earned him an audience with George III and a watch from the Prince of Wales.

Two views of Westmill, near Buntingford and one of the prettiest villages in the county. As well as the water pump, there is a village green bordered by attractive cottages and a church that is Saxon in origin. A little to the west in Wakeley a single farm is all that survives of a lost village. Nearby at Cherry Green is Button Snap, a whitewashed thatched cottage once bequeathed to that great lover of Hertfordshire, Charles Lamb (1775-1834), who mentions the cottage in his essay, 'My First Play'. 'When I journeyed down to take possession. . .' he wrote, 'I strode with larger paces over my allotment of three quarters of an acre, with its commodious mansion in the midst, with the feeling of an English freeholder that all betwixt sky and centre was my own.'

THE CHILTERNS AND
THE WEST

THE CHILTERNS AND THE WEST

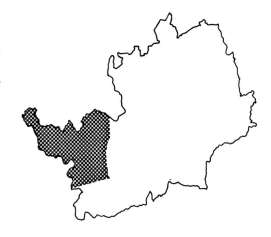

Western Hertfordshire juts like an arm through the gentle Chilterns, that low range of wooded hills that curls from south-west to north-east along the county's border. In the gap thus created nestles Tring, and on the Chilterns themselves is the 4,000 acre Ashridge Park, which the National Trust opens to the public – the one-time home of the Duke of Bridgewater, the so-called 'canal duke', father of inland navigation.

One of the results of the duke's pioneering work, the Grand Union Canal, runs through this corner of the county. Towards the end of the eighteenth century it brought the benefits of the Industrial Revolution south into Hertfordshire from the Midlands. But, with its former commercial duty done, the canal now lures thousands of pleasure seekers to its waters – either anglers or the canal boat enthusiasts chugging along in their often picturesque, often ageing, craft.

The largest town in west Hertfordshire, Hemel Hempstead, was one of the first new towns to be built after the Second World War. It integrates the old town, where St Mary's church – one of thirty parish churches in the area, many partly or wholly medieval – proclaims its presence with the tallest lead spire in all Europe.

Perhaps Berkhamsted has a prior claim to being the area's town most deeply immersed in history, for it witnessed the event that was to set the course for all other English towns for centuries. Here William the Conqueror was offered the English crown at the Castle – now a ruin looking out over the canal and river.

Previous page Little Manor, Frithsden, a charming sixteenth-century house faced with an unusual form of decorative pargeting – using gypsum instead of the customary plaster. The square panels were put on roughcast during a restoration in 1879. An unusual building next to the garden is a chapel, built in 1835, and a small churchyard, which was de-consecrated in the 1950s.

A child plays among the graves in Aldbury churchyard.

Behind a timbered cottage is the medieval church at Aldbury, near Ashridge, on the edge of the Chilterns.

Summer comes to Ashridge. The towering granite Doric column of the Bridgewater Monument was erected in 1832 in honour of the 3rd Duke of Bridgewater. He was nicknamed the 'Canal Duke' because he built ten miles of canal over an aqueduct between his coal-mine at Worsley and Manchester in 1762, thus passing into history as the originator of British inland navigation. His pioneering work was followed up in canals such as the Grand Union, built in 1793, which runs through west Hertfordshire on its way to Birmingham. The Duke occupied the original Ashridge house, but unfortunately allowed it to fall into decay. The present house was built between 1808 and 1820 and is now a management training college.

The 4,000 acres of the Ashridge estate on the slopes of the Chilterns are a glorious mixture of woodland, commons and open space which spread from west Hertfordshire over the border into Buckinghamshire. Now in the care of the National Trust, Ashridge is rich in wild-life, including 300 fallow and muntjac deer, and even a species of edible dormouse called the glis glis.

Stallholders and customers at a market on a disused airfield at Bovingdon on the edge of the Chilterns, near Hemel Hempstead.

Flamstead, near Markyate, where apart from those in St Albans Cathedral the thirteenth-century wall paintings in St Leonard's church are said to be the best in the county. To the west of the village at Beechwood was where a huge crowd watched John Gully beat Bob Gregson in 27 rounds in an hour-and-a-quarter at a marathon prize fight in 1808. Prize fighting was then illegal, but the promoter, Sir John Sebright, a member of a well-known local family, was a magistrate and needed the money, so no action was taken.

Three photographs of the Hertfordshire Show. For nearly 200 years, since 1801, the Hertfordshire Show has been the biggest agricultural event in the county's calendar. The Show takes place annually over the two days before the spring Bank Holiday on its own 80-acre site on the A5183 near Redbourn. Among typical events are international show-jumping, the showing of heavy horses in hand, classes for exhibiting rare breeds of livestock and poultry, sheepdog trials and a three-day dog show.

Narrowboats crowd the lock on the Grand Union Canal at Berkhamsted. The Canal opened in 1793 and is still navigable. There is now a 'green corridor' along its towpath, so that ramblers can walk the 145 miles from Little Venice in London to Birmingham's Gas Street Basin.

Berkhamsted Castle, near White Hill, was the scene of one of the most important events in British history, though all that remains today is the outer bailey and the mound, or motte. After their defeat at the Battle of Hastings in 1066 the Saxons realised that London was about to fall to William of Normandy, whose forces then encircled it. To avoid bloodshed, and surrendering to the inevitable, a deputation of Saxon nobles met William at Berkhamsted Castle and offered him the throne of England. Later, the castle became the favourite home of Edward, Prince of Wales (1330-1376),the Black Prince. The clerk of works at Berkhamsted in 1389 was the poet Geoffrey Chaucer.

Vineyard workers at Frithsden, near Hemel Hempstead, cocoon the maturing vines with nets to protect the grapes from birds. The three-acre vineyard, founded by Peter and Anne Latchford, is planted on a south-facing slope in the foothills of the Chilterns, where the flinty loam on chalk produces a fragrant and fruity wine. The Domesday Book of 1086 mentions 45 English vineyards, most of them monastic, where vines were grown both to raise revenue and supply Communion wine.

Looking from Redbourn Common towards the village of the 'reedy stream' – the medieval meaning of Redbourn's name. The stream is the River Ver, which fringes it. Dr Henry Stephens, the inventor of Stephens Ink, lived here, and the village is claimed to have the oldest cricket team in the county, dating from 1666.

The calm waters of the Tring Reservoirs, havens for birds and fish near Wilstone.

The spire of St Mary's church, Hemel Hempstead – at 200 feet high the tallest lead spire in Europe – appears to be competing with the 18-storey Kodak building, the highest building in Hemel Hempstead. St Mary's, which stands in the High Street in the old town, is the most complete Norman church in the county, except for St Albans Cathedral. The old town and its High Street are exceptionally attractive.

Bowlers in Gadebridge Park, Hemel Hempstead, and *(below right)* a bus passing through the mixture of mature and young trees that give Gadebridge Park its delightful leafy character.

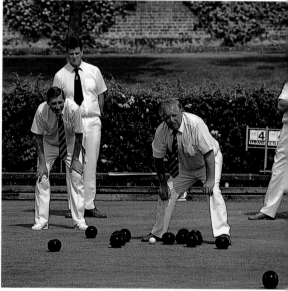

Traffic thickens up on the M1 on its 19-mile route through Hertfordshire from Junction 5, near Watford, to Junction 10, just south of Luton. Vehicle speeds are faster on the M1 than the M25 and the accident rate is twice as high. 'Too fast and too close' is a principal cause of motorway accidents, says Sergeant Roger Barrett, of Hertfordshire Constabulary's Motorway Division Headquarters near Watford. The M1 was Britain's first motorway, and the Hertfordshire section of the original two lane motorway between London and Birmingham opened in 1966.

Tring's nineteenth-century Louisa Cottages, built as almshouses and dated 1893 and 1901, were the work of William Huckvale, who also gave the High Street its late-Victorian character, and was architect to the Rothschild family of Tring Park. The 2nd Baron Rothschild founded the Zoological Museum, which opened to the public in 1892 and stands at the junction of Akeman Street and Park Street: it is now an annexe of the London Natural History Museum. In his enthusiasm for animals, Rothschild once had a team of zebras haul a family coach along Piccadilly.

ST ALBANS AND HATFIELD

ST ALBANS AND HATFIELD

This part of Hertfordshire bears the imprints of two eras – the Roman and the Elizabethan.

Remains dating from the Roman occupation have been found in many parts of the county – there's even a bath-house under the A1 – but by far the most important have been in the Roman city of Verulamium, which became St Albans. Indeed, flint taken from the walls of Verulamium was re-used by the medieval masons who built the Cathedral. Little remains of Verulamium itself; it is a ghost city, now a public park, but fragments of flint wall and the outlines of gateways and buildings, and the ruins of the nearby Roman theatre, remain as a spur to the imagination.

St Albans Cathedral, the principal landmark, stands on the presumed site of the execution of Alban, a Roman soldier. Its earliest architecture is Norman, but its styles run the gamut of the medieval, though the twentieth century is represented in the modern Chapter House, opened by the Queen in 1982, and the delicate stained-glass in the Laporte Rose Window.

A few miles to the east is Hatfield House, the home of the influential Cecil family for centuries, where Elizabeth I was told of her accession to the throne while sitting under a tree in the garden. The entire house and gardens are steeped in its Elizabethan and Jacobean atmosphere, as is nearby Old Hatfield, which still preserves its village character. Meanwhile, there are the newer Hatfield, and the A1(M) which divides Hertfordshire in two like the vein in a leaf, as bustling reminders of the second Elizabeth.

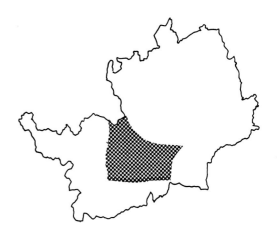

Previous page Folly Arch, at North Mymms near Potters Bar, is an eighteenth-century brick folly built by Sir Jeremy Sambrooke, who also built the Battle of Barnet memorial at Hadley. The arch leads nowhere, and although it may once have served as a gateway its prime function was to act as a decorative feature on the skyline. Sir Jeremy's house, Gobions, has been pulled down, and now only its lake remains. Sir Thomas More (1478-1535), the great Chancellor of England who was executed after falling foul of Henry VIII over the annulment of his marriage to Catherine of Aragon, once owned a house near the arch.

A visitor's umbrella vies for colour with some of the rich collection of roses at Bone Hill, Chiswell Green, near St Albans. The 12 acres of the Gardens of the Rose, headquarters of the Royal National Rose Society, Britain's oldest and biggest specialist horticultural society, contain one of the most important collections of roses in the world: 30,000 in 1,700 varieties. New roses come from all over the world to the trial grounds at Bone Hill to be rigorously assessed over three years for their value as garden plants. Highlight of the Gardens' year is the British Rose Festival, held early in July, when roses are at the peak of their first flush. But the gardens are open from mid-June to late October.

Harpenden is one of Hertfordshire's most attractive and pleasant towns. Its leafy character is typified by the High Street, which is divided down the middle by greens and trees. There are several noteworthy older buildings in or near the town. St Nicholas's church is mainly Victorian, but the plastered-flint tower is dated 1470 and there is a font from around 1200. One of the most interesting houses is Flowton Priory, a delightful timbered Tudor house, which once stood in Ipswich, and was brought to Harpenden in 1928, brick by brick, and rebuilt. The sevententh-century Rothamsted Manor is the one-time home of Sir John Bennet Lawes (1814-1900), founder of the Rothamsted Agricultural Research Centre, which has achieved world-wide fame for its work on crop improvement.

Harpenden Common.

Wearing his customary unusual line in headgear, Larry Laird has worked as a gardener and hedger at Hatfield House since 1980. He became Hertfordshire's champion hedge layer in 1986. The decorations on his hat are his own wood-carvings of horses, dogs and birds. A self-taught carver, he produces ornaments, walking sticks and shepherd's crooks in answer to requests from all over the world.

The Eight Bells Inn, in Old Hatfield village, is associated with Charles Dickens, who used it in *Oliver Twist* as the taproom where, after murdering Nancy, Bill Sikes starts talking to a pedlar who innocently commented on the blood stains on Sikes's hat. Dickens was a regular visitor to Hertfordshire, on one occasion coming to report a serious fire at Hatfield House for the *Morning Chronicle*, and it could have been then that he visited the Eight Bells.

No family has played a more prominent role in the affairs of state than the Cecils, whose home has been at Hatfield House for nearly four hundred years. Although Jacobean, the house is Elizabethan in style – its plan is the letter E, for Elizabeth I – and was completed in 1612. The earliest part is the Old Palace, finished in about 1497, and it was here that the young Princess Elizabeth was kept in seclusion before she became Queen in 1558. The years she spent at Hatfield haunt the house still, for amongst its relics are her silk stockings, gardening hat and gloves, and it was while sitting under an oak tree in the grounds that she was first told of her accession to the throne. Her first action was to send for William Cecil, later Lord Burghley (1520-1598), whom she made her Chief Minister, and she held her first Council as Queen in the hall of the Old Palace. James I, Elizabeth's successor, did not favour the Palace; he preferred Theobalds (at Cheshunt), then occupied by Burghley's son, Robert Cecil – later to become 1st Earl of Salisbury – and both agreed to an exchange. Thus began the Cecils' centuries-long association with Hatfield.

In the little church of St Etheldreda at the top of Fore Street, Old Hatfield, stands the imposing white marble tomb of Robert Cecil, the 1st Earl of Salisbury, who became Queen Elizabeth I's Secretary of State – equivalent to Prime Minister – and died in 1612. The earl, in effigy on a black marble slab, wears his Garter robes and holds his wand of office as Lord High Treasurer to James I, the post he held at his death. The slab is supported by four kneeling figures: Prudence, Justice, Fortitude and Temperance. The church and its churchyard are also the burial place of two other Prime Ministers – Viscount Melbourne, Queen Victoria's guide and mentor, who is remembered by a simple plaque on a pillar near the pulpit, and the 3rd Marquess of Salisbury, three times Prime Minister in Victoria's reign, who died in 1903 and lies in the family burial ground to the east of the church.

As befits a family that originally engaged that great plantsman John Tradescant, the gardens at Hatfield House are one of its greatest glories. The gardens today owe much to the present Marchioness of Salisbury, who has used the plants that would have been known to her Jacobean ancestors to create a series of small intimate gardens. Shown here are part of the East Gardens, with their parterres, summer-flowering shrubs and herbaceous plants. The double row of clipped evergreen oaks, *Quercus ilex*, was specially imported from Italy and planted in 1977. They are not reliably hardy and took 10 years to grow and train.

Right A view of the West Gardens from the roof of Hatfield House with Hatfield in the distance. In the foreground is the Privy Garden, with its lily pool and fountain, the work of Lady Gwendolen Cecil, youngest daughter of Queen Victoria's Prime Minister, the 3rd Marquess of Salisbury.

The 'Wooden Wonder'. Smartly dressed in its original livery, the prototype De Havilland Mosquito at the Mosquito Aircraft Museum at Salisbury Hall, London Colney, near St Albans. The twin-engined fighter/bomber was made almost entirely of wood, hence its nickname. The planes were built at Hatfield throughout the Second World War and most famously saw service in the Pathfinder force led by Air Vice Marshal Donald Bennett. A total of 7,700 Mosquitos were built. The first was flown in 1941 and the last were taken out of service in 1958.

Right An aerial photograph of the Cathedral and Abbey Church of St Alban, St Albans. The Cathedral marks the site of the execution in AD 209 of Alban, a Roman soldier who was martyred for disobeying an edict against Christians by sheltering a priest. The first monastic church was built by AD 300, during the Roman occupation of Britain, overlooking the Roman city of Verulamium, and flints and stones from Verulamium are incorporated into the Cathedral walls. The bulk of the Cathedral was built shortly after the Norman Conquest by its first Norman abbot, Paul of Caen. The Abbey was dissolved following the Dissolution of the Monasteries in 1539, after which all but the church and gatehouse were demolished. The church was bought by the townspeople as their parish church for £400, and in 1877 it became the cathedral for the new diocese of St Albans.

Salisbury Hall, a moated 17th-century manor house near London Colney, has had a mixture of residents during its history. Nell Gwynne, Charles II's mistress, lived in a cottage nearby, where she forced the king to give one of her children a title by threatening to drop it into the moat, 30 feet below. 'Spare the Duke of St Albans!' cried the king, mentioning the first place name to enter his head. Salisbury Hall formed part of a bigger house built by Sir John Cuttes, Henry VIII's Treasurer. Others to have lived in the Hall include Winston Churchill and his mother, Sir Nigel Gresley, the LNER locomotive engineer, and – during the war – De Havilland's aircraft designers.

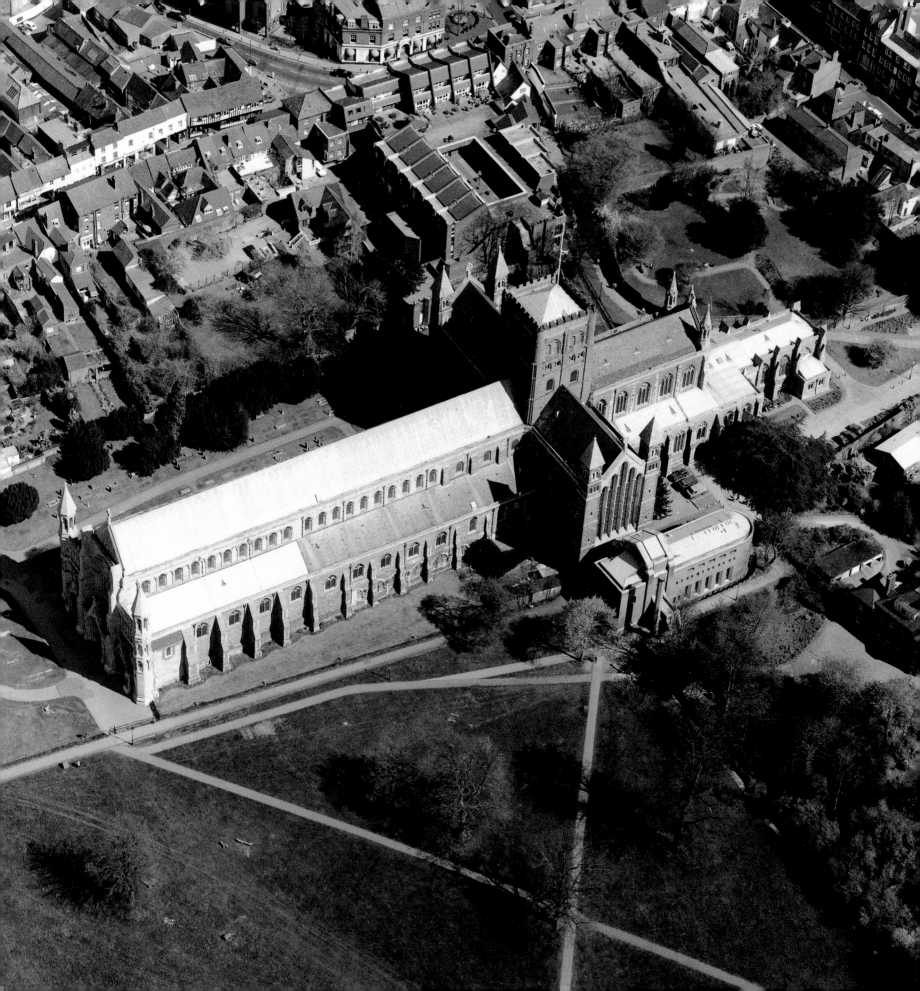

The tower of St Albans Cathedral from the south-west. The 144 feet tower was built between 1077 and 1093 with bricks taken from the Roman town of Verulamium.

The Norman arch leading into the north transept of St Albans Cathedral, and the modern Laporte Rose Window, presented to the Cathedral by Laporte plc to mark its centenary and dedicated and unveiled by the Princess of Wales in 1989.

Top Fishpool Street, St Albans, a part of the city where many of the houses can be traced back to the sixteenth and seventeenth centuries. The street is near what was the gateway to the Abbey, and owes its name to the fishponds belonging to the monks.

Above Customers reflected in a mirror on one of the stalls of the market in St Peter's Street and the Market Place, St Albans.

Right The Clock Tower in French Row, St Albans, which offers visitors impressive views of the city. It was built as a Curfew Tower between 1402 and 1411. An Eleanor Cross, erected by Edward I in memory of his wife, Eleanor of Castile, used to stand nearby. French Row was formerly Cobblers Row, and was renamed because in 1216 French prisoners were confined there.

Opposite page The Roman theatre at Verulamium from the air.

Unaware of the camera's all-seeing eye peeping through a gap in the Roman wall, a girl plays as Roman children must surely have done on this same spot seventeen hundred years ago in Verulamium. The public park is laid out on the site of the Roman city and is fringed by the little River Ver. In a corner of the park is Verulamium Museum, which contains many Roman remains excavated from the city, including some magnificent tessellated pavements.

Schoolchildren studying the only completely excavated Roman theatre in England, which stands a few hundred yards west of Verulamium itself. The theatre was discovered in 1847, filled in, then re-excavated and opened to the public in the 1930s. It had tiered seating – surviving now as grassy banks – as well as the stage, dressing rooms and an arena. Some of the Roman shops that once stood near the theatre were burned down in AD 60 by Boudicca, queen of the Iceni. A figure of Venus, discovered in the 1950s in the basement of a bronzeworker's shop on the theatre site, can be seen in Verulamium Museum nearby.

Windsurfers and Canada geese add a splash of colour to Stanborough Park, near Welwyn Garden City. The two lakes at the Park were excavated in 1946 to provide watersports, dinghy-sailing and canoeing. They have also become a haven for wildlife, with nature trails and a conservation area managed by the Herts and Middlesex Wildlife Trust among the willow woodland and reed marshes that surround the lakes.

HERTFORD AND THE
LEA VALLEY

HERTFORD AND THE LEA VALLEY

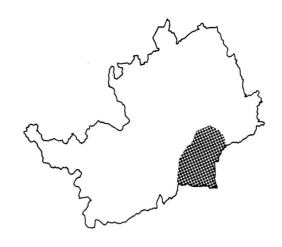

Hertford, the county's capital, prides itself on being only 25 miles from London and within easy reach of three motorways. Despite this it has an unmistakable country town atmosphere, helped along by its shopping precinct, fine old buildings, cattle market and wide reputation as a centre for antiques.

Its very proximity to London is no doubt why, throughout history, royalty – and even governments – have on occasion been accommodated in the Castle; for example, by Queen Elizabeth I at the time of the plague. Even as far back as the seventh century, Hertford was the setting for an historic meeting between church leaders. And the oldest purpose-built Friends' Meeting House in the world, built in about 1669 and still in use.

The River Lea, having crossed the county from the west, passes through Hertford on its way south to the Thames via Broxbourne. Because of its loamy nature, Lea Valley soil is highly fertile – an ideal growing medium for salad crops, hence the prolific 'hatching' on the Ordnance Survey map indicating nurseries.

Previous page The gateway of Rye House, near Hoddesdon. The original house has long been demolished, but when built in 1443 it was one of the earliest examples of a brick-built building in the country. But the House is best remembered for the Rye House Plot, an attempt to assassinate Charles II and his brother the Duke of York (later James II) in 1683. The conspirators, who included the then tenant of the House, Richard Rumbold, intended to ambush the royal party on its way back to London from the Newmarket Races. The attempt failed because of the king's premature return to London following a fire at the racecourse. The forty conspirators, among whom was Charles II's illegitimate son the Duke of Monmouth, were eventually betrayed, and all were either exiled, imprisoned or executed.

A summer's day, blue skies, and village cricket. A match in progress at Bayford, south of Hertford. (*Opposite page*) The scorers enjoying their tea.

But foreign competition put many growers out of business in the 1980s, and much glass has given way to garden centres: bedding plants, seeds, implements, pots and plants. At Crews Hill, near Cuffley, for example, a half-mile of nurseries has been turned over entirely to garden centres selling plants and shrubs bought in for public sale, but not grown on site. Supermarkets and high street stores now also sell what nurserymen would once sell direct to the public.

The rivers themselves have changed too. Within living memory, commercial barges were a familiar sight on the Lea, but road transport has long since displaced them. Renewed life for the Lea, however, came in 1967 with the creation of the Lea Valley Regional Park, a vast leisure area stretching for 23 miles from the East End of London to Ware. Apart from fishing, and the use of canal boats, many of the amenities are concentrated at Broxbourne, which has facilities for rowing, motor-boating and swimming (in a lido), complete with the latest trimmings such as a wave machine, sauna and solarium, not forgetting the inevitable caravan park.

And what of the New River, that lifeline provided by Sir Hugh Myddelton? Even today, after nearly 400 years, it is still helping to slake London's thirst for fresh water.

Pleasure boats and commercial barges on the River Lea near Broxbourne. The Lea rises near Luton, becomes navigable at Hertford Canal Basin, near Bull Plain, Hertford, then winds southwards down Hertfordshire's eastern boundary before finally flowing into the Thames near the Isle of Dogs.

Right An angler fishing the River Lea at Hertford.

A detail of Temple Bar, designed by Sir Christopher Wren, and which now stands alone in a rather woebegone state at Theobald's, near Cheshunt, where James I died. The monument was one of London's greatest landmarks. It stood where the Strand and Fleet Street join until 1878, when it was dismantled stone by stone because its arches were too narrow to accommodate the increase in horse-drawn traffic. It was bought by the brewer, Sir Henry Meux, and re-erected at Theobald's, where it has stood ever since. It has sadly suffered badly from neglect, and its planned restoration and return to the City, to stand near Wren's greater glory, St Paul's Cathedral, as yet remain a dream.

Below A century-old street lamp from Brompton in Kensington, one of nearly a hundred street lamps in the Museum of Street Lighting in Great Amwell, near Ware. The collection has been assembled by a local lamp manufacturing company, Concrete Utilities, of Lower Road, and can be seen by appointment.

The Postern Gate of Hertford Castle, built by the Normans on the bank of River Lea, probably within a Saxon stronghold. The handsome brick gatehouse is a relic of the Castle rebuilt by Edward IV in 1463 and enlarged in George III's time, and is now used as offices by Hertford Town Council and East Herts District Council. Hertford was originally laid-out as a fortified town by Alfred the Great's son Edward the Elder in AD 912. The mound in the north-east corner of the gardens, by the River Lea, is all that remains of the original Norman motte-and-bailey castle. In 1170 Henry II replaced a timber palisade with a curtain wall of flint and stone, and it is the ruins of this wall that are visible today.

Weir Cottage, in the grounds of Hertford Castle.

The statue of the county's symbolic stag which
dominates Parliament Square, Hertford.

Fore Street, Hertford, whose fine old buildings include this seventeenth-century one faced with decorative plasterwork, or pargeting. Next to it, with the clock, is the eighteenth-century Shire Hall, now housing the Magistrates' Courts.

Below left The old covered market which has stood in Market Street, Hertford, since 1889.

The clock tower and frontage of McMullen's Brewery in Cowbridge, off Old Cross, Hertford, have been familiar features there since 1891, although the company – the only family brewer in Hertfordshire – was founded in 1827.

Below Pockets of hops being poured into the coppers in McMullen's Brewery, adding flavour to the beer.

Left Rescuers in Rye Meads Nature and RSPB Reserve tend an injured swan that has hit overhead electricity wires. The reserves adjoin Rye Park and cover what is left of flood meadows in the Lea Valley. Snipe, corn buntings, yellowhammers and sedge warblers can be seen.

Below Hertford's cattle market, in Caxton Hill, is one of the town's oldest, if these days less busy, institutions. For 500 years it carried on business near Fore Street, then moved to Ram Yard and, in 1950, to Caxton Hill. Its next move will be to Hoe Lane, Ware.

Lettuces being cut and packed ready for despatch at the Limes Nursery, Cheshunt. The rich alluvial sandy loam in the Lea Valley, particularly near the river itself, has long made it an excellent growing area for salad crops and bedding plants. The many nurseries in the Valley flourished as London grew and the railways linked even the smallest of them to Covent Garden Market. More recently, cheaper imports, many of them subsidised, have led to many nurserymen being forced to close.

A distant view of Woolmers, a handsome eighteenth-century house built next to the Lea, near Hertingfordbury. The house, which has a colonnade dating from 1821-23, is seen here from the top of Stratton's Folly, Little Berkhampsted. Woolmers was built by the Biddulph family, who lived there until 1798. The next owner was Samuel Whitbread, the Whig politician and son of the founder of the brewing company. The Countess of Strathmore lived there for many years, and since 1949 it has been occupied by the Lucas family.

Stratton's Folly, the five-storey tower that looks out over the village of Little Berkhampsted, was built in 1789 as an observatory, for its owner, John Stratton, a retired admiral, to see ships plying up and down the Thames – a futile exercise.

Below The view from the top of Stratton's Folly.

The head of the New River at Chadwell Springs, Ware, which originally flowed 38 miles to take fresh water to London. The river is hardly 'new', having been cut by Sir Hugh Myddelton in 1613. He was encouraged by James I, and his determination and vision earned him a baronetcy, but lost him a fortune.

Two miles down-river from Chadwell, on an island at Great Amwell, are two commemorative stones. The one shown bears verses reputedly from the pen of the Quaker poet John Scott, of Ware – a hymn of praise for the benefit of the New River:

Amwell, perpetual by thy stream
Nor e'er thy springs be less
Which thousands drink who never dream
Whence flows the boon they bless.

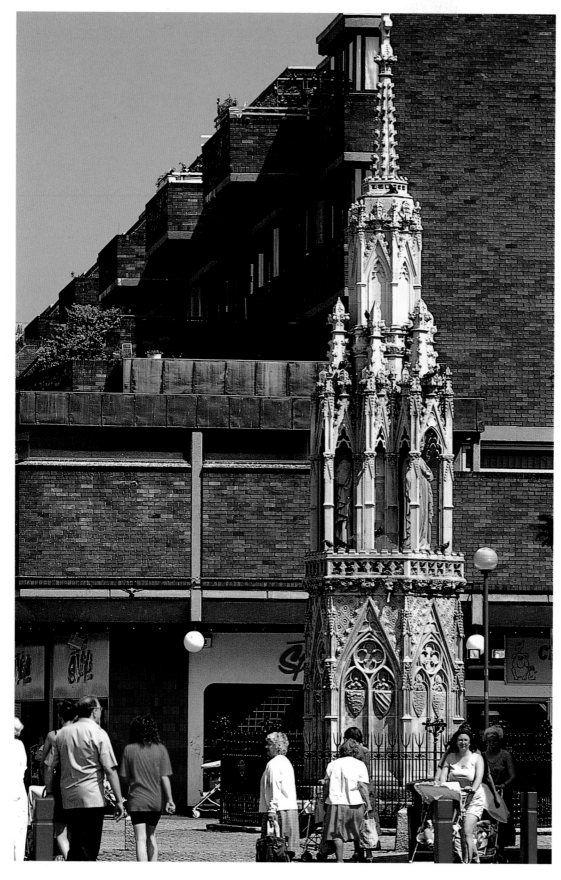

The Waltham Cross in the town named after it. The Cross is one of only three remaining out of the twelve that Edward I erected in 1291 after the death of his much-loved queen, Eleanor of Castile, at Harby in Nottinghamshire. The Eleanor crosses stood at all the places where her coffin rested on the journey from Harby to Westminster Abbey. Only a few hundred yards away – but over the Essex border – is Waltham Abbey, where King Harold prayed before the Battle of Hastings, and where he is thought to be buried.

WATFORD AND THE SOUTH

WATFORD AND THE SOUTH

Southern Hertfordshire has probably experienced more change in the past thirty years than anywhere else in the county. In 1965, Hertfordshire lost Barnet to Greater London, Middlesex was abolished as an administrative county, and Potters Bar, traditionally part of Middlesex, was attached to Hertfordshire.

Loyalties have not faded; even now neat signs stating 'County of Middlesex' can be seen at county boundaries. But in 1986 came another change – one which probably affected Hertfordshire people more in a practical sense: the opening of the M25. There was, of course, a loss of agricultural land, but it is not overstating the case to say that the lives of many people in South Hertfordshire have been immeasurably improved by the M25. Not only has it become a key to quicker travel in all directions, but a relief for many a beleaguered town centre. But for it, Potters Bar High Street, for example, would still be choked with heavy lorries from the A1 bound for London's Docklands.

One of the biggest towns to benefit has been Watford, just south of the M25. Watford has successfully striven for years to make industry's presence palatable by insisting on good design and retaining plenty of open spaces.

Borehamwood, which became one of London's overspill areas in the 1950s, has fared less well. Though its light industry thrives, the balmy days of prosperity producing British films are a fond memory. Today, the studios maintain only a tenuous toehold with television work, accompanied by dreams of a film revival.

There is water in plenty here, with reservoirs at Aldenham, and at Watford and Rickmansworth the Grand Union Canal. Indeed, Rickmansworth's medieval name 'Rykemeresworth' means 'rich town between the waters' – the Rivers Colne, Gade and Chess.

Previous page Weeping willows line the little River Gade in Cassiobury Park, providing a peaceful oasis near the centre of Watford. The park is shared between golf, a public open space and a marshy, wooded nature reserve managed by the Herts and Middlesex Wildlife Trust. What were once watercress beds are now home to dozens of species of dragonfly, molluscs and fish.

A narrowboat approaches one of the many bridges crossing the Grand Union Canal near Watford.

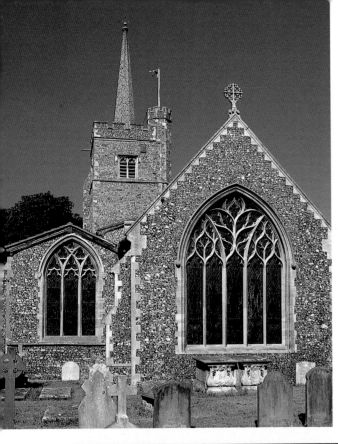

The well-proportioned thirteenth-century tower of St John the Baptist, Aldenham, east of Watford.

Below Early this century the large group of Tudor-style brick buildings in The Avenue, Bushey, served as the Royal Masonic School. Since 1972, however, it has been the campus of the International University, Europe, one of several American universities in the London area used by students the world over.

Strawberry pickers at Cattlegate Farm, Crews Hill, one of scores of farms in the county feeding the public's passion for pick-your-own produce. Throughout the summer, thousands of Londoners flock out into Hertfordshire at weekends in search of fresh fruit and fresh air – and some exercise while picking. Hertfordshire's county boundary with the London Borough of Enfield cuts straight through the middle of Cattlegate Farm.

A student pilot takes off near Elstree Reservoir
under instruction with Cabair at the London
School of Flying, Elstree Aerodrome, a popular
venue for trainee fliers.

Right In silent contrast, a hot-air balloon passes
over parkland near Aldenham.

St Paul's Church and the war memorial at Hunton Bridge, just north of the M25. The church was built in 1865, and was described by Sir Nikolaus Pevsner as 'ambitious for so small a parish.'

Wrongdoers caught in Shenley in the eighteenth and nineteenth centuries cooled off for a spell in this curious domed lock-up. Shenley Cage, as it is known, is made of concrete-coated brick, and has salutary warnings inscribed on the outside walls: 'Be sober, be vigilant' and 'Do well and fear not'. In the churchyard is the grave of Nicholas Hawksmoor, Sir Christopher Wren's assistant and friend, who also designed and built London churches.

Sergeant Paul Pedlingham and W.P.C. Lorna Adams of the motorway division of Hertfordshire Constabulary, keep watch on the M25 where it heads west between Potters Bar and London Colney. The entire circuit of the M25, which opened in 1986, is about 187km (117 miles), of which about 41km (26 miles) slices across the southern part of the county between West Hyde in the west to just beyond Waltham Cross in the east. The M25 is a much safer road than the M1, which also passes through Hertfordshire: the M25's accident rate is half that of the M1, with 2.6 accidents per kilometre per year, compared with the M1's 5.7 – mainly because congestion reduces the average speed of M25 traffic.

A towpath walker's view of the underside of the M25, where it crosses the Grand Union Canal south of King's Langley.

Typical late-nineteenth century semi-detached houses in Upper Station Road, Radlett. Radlett owes its growth to its position on Watling Street, once the main Roman road to the north-west of England.

Cottages and riders on the green at Sarratt, near the Hertfordshire border with Buckinghamshire, north-west of Watford.

The Green, Letchmore Heath, and the Three
Horseshoes Inn, part of which is two hundred
years old and was originally a forge.

A canal boat on the Grand Union Canal near
Rickmansworth.

Narrowboats, an often colourful feature of the Grand Union Canal, wait their turn at a lock near Croxley Green, Watford.

Bathers take a cooling dip in the Ironbridge Lock in Cassiobury Park.

A pattern of rooftops at the Harlequin Centre, an indoor shopping complex at Watford, whose arched windows disguise a multi-storey car park.

Below right Inside the Centre, amidst the escalators and arcades, Atlas shoulders a different burden.

Shops and a decorative pool in The Parade, near the Town Hall, Watford. The town was founded on brewing and printing: brewing as far back as 1619, though now the last brewer has gone. Printing still thrives, along with the processing of ink and paper, and Watford today is very much a 'high tech' town, at the forefront of electronic and electrical engineering. You have to look for old Watford, but it is there. For instance, the chancel in St Mary's church dates back to the thirteenth century. My own personal favourite is the Palace Theatre in Clarendon Road, which opened in 1908. It may not impress from the outside, but the interior is an Edwardian delight, and one can mingle with the ghosts of the great performers who have walked out onto its stage – from Chaplin to Marie Lloyd, from Stan Laurel to Bob Hope, from George Robey to Gracie Fields.

The Bedford Almshouses, St Mary's Road, Watford, founded in 1580. They are situated in the churchyard on the west side of the High Street with the eighteenth-century Mrs Elizabeth Fuller Free School.

A bumper harvest of chimneys and rooftops among the smaller houses in an older part of Watford. Here in the south, Hertfordshire is at its most urban, and in places almost runs into Greater London.

THE PHOTOGRAPHS

Virtually all of the photographs in this book were taken specially for it over a year in an effort to try and evoke a portrait of Hertfordshire as it is today. I must in all truth admit that when I was first asked to photograph the county I was slightly hesitant. My preconceptions had made Hertfordshire flat, intensively farmed, over-populated in many places by both man and machine, and unlikely to be blessed by even the occasional dramatic sunrise or sunset. Thus armed with a basket of excuses, I began a 100-day, 6,000-mile journey of discovery that was as rewarding and surprising as any I have made.

Hertfordshire's character is not obvious. It has to be discovered along the leafy lanes of the south-east; in the quiet, still villages surrounding the major towns of the south-west, and, not least, in the gently rolling hills of the north. I hope these photographs reflect the true nature of the county and its people, for their warmth and generosity made my year in Hertfordshire a memorable one.

For the record, no use was made of filters, flash or tripod for any of the photographs. My only luxury was a Leica R system of four bodies and superb lenses, ranging from 28mm to 250mm. I used Fujichrome Velvia film throughout.

I would like to thank Erica Brown for being there every time it counts, and dedicate my contribution to the book to Nancy and Bill Urwin of Carlisle.

JOHN HODDER

ACKNOWLEDGEMENTS

Very many people have helped create this book, and our thanks are due to them all. First and foremost, there are the people of Hertfordshire depicted in the book, either wittingly or unwittingly. The research has meant contacting many people for advice and assistance, including the public relations departments of Hertfordshire's many borough, district and town councils, all of whom we sincerely thank. The encouragement of the booksellers throughout the county has been most welcome: without their support books such as this would be all but impossible.

We are particularly grateful to Brendan Quinlan of Aerofilms Ltd, Borehamwood, for his help in supplying the three aerial photographs; of Letchworth, St Albans Cathedral, and the Roman theatre at Verulamium.

Among those who have helped us we must mention the following, and extend our gratitude: Kevin Boldison, of Patchetts, Hilfield Lane, Patchetts Green, near Aldenham; Mike Brennan, of Hertfordshire County Council's Transportation Dept; British Road Federation; Cattlegate Farm, Crews Hill; Brian Crozier, of Norris & Duvall, Hertford; Louise Dobbs for the colour map; Martin Douglas, of Concrete Utilities Ltd, Gt Amwell; Colin Heathcote, of Cabair, the London School of Flying, Elstree Aerodrome; Lynn Warren, The Henry Moore Foundation, Perry Green; Fiona HIll, of Sandon; Shinichi Hori, of Salisbury Hall, London Colney; Irvin Great Britain Ltd., Letchworth; International University, Europe, of Bushey; Len Kerswill, of Watford; The Estate Office, Knebworth House; Bob Laurenson, Hertfordshire Show; Limes Nursery, Cheshunt; Mrs L.A. Lucas, of Woolmers, Hertingfordbury; Colonel Douglas McCord, Curator, Hatfield House; the dependable technicians of Metro Photographic, London; The Mosquito Aircraft Museum, Salisbury Hall, London Colney; National Farmers' Union, Hertfordshire branch; Sgt Paul Pedlingham and Wpc Lorna Adams, and Sgt Roger Barrett, Motorway Division HQ, Hertfordshire Constabulary; Thane Prince, *Daily Telegraph*; John Rochford and staff, of Hertford Tourist Information Office; Denis Ruttledge, of McMullens of Hertford Ltd, Hertford; staff at Stanborough Park, Welwyn Garden City; Roger Sygrave, of Capel Manor Horticultural Centre, Enfield; Gillian Thornton, of Harpenden; staff of the White Horse Hotel, Hertingfordbury; Captains Rod Wood and Richard Watt, of Cabair Helicopters, Elstree Aerodrome.

Finally, our thanks to our publisher, David Burnett, who has not allowed his seemingly inexhaustible supply of patience to outweigh his determination, and to his assistant, Elizabeth Dean, for her unfailing help and courtesy.

JOHN HODDER AND JOHN LUCAS

INDEX

Aldenham 4, 110, 112
Aldbury 60, 61, 62
Ardeley 30
Ashridge 62, 63
Ashwell 31
Ayot St Lawrence 12

Baldock 32, 33, 34
Barley 36
Bayford 92, 93
Bedwell 23
Benington 29, 36, 37
Berkhamsted 66
Berkhamsted Castle 67
Bishop's Stortford 38
Bone Hill 75
Bovingdon 64
Braughing 39
Brocket Hall 15
Broxbourne 94
Bucklersbury 13
Buntingford 39
Bushey 110

Cassiobury Park 107, 122
Chadwell 105
Chadwell Springs 104
Cheshunt 95, 101
Chilterns 61, 64
Chiswell Green 75
Clothall 35
Crews Hill 111
Croxley Green 120, 121

Digswell Viaduct 13
Elstree Aerodrome 112

Fairlands Valley Park 24
Flamstead 64
Frithsden 59, 68
Furneux Pelham 41, 46
Furneux Pelham Hall 40

Grand Union Canal 66, 109, 116, 119, 121
Great Amwell 95, 105
Great Hormead 41

Harpenden 76
Hatfield House 78, 80, 81
Hemel Hempstead 70
Hertford 94, 97, 98, 99, 100
Hertford Castle 96
Hertfordshire Show 65
Hitchin 13, 14
Hunton Bridge 114

Kelshall 44, 45, 50, 51
King's Walden 10, 17
Knebworth House 18, 19, 25

Letchmore Heath 118
Letchworth 20, 21, 22
Little Hormead 42, 43
London Colney 82

Much Hadham 52

New River 104, 105
North Mymms 73

Old Hatfield 77, 79
Old Welwyn, frontispiece, 26

Perry Green 53

Radlett 117
Redbourn 68
Rickmansworth 119
River Lea 15, 94
Royston 47, 48
Rye House 91

Salisbury Hall 82
Sandon 54
Sarratt 117
Sawbridgeworth 54
Shenley 115
St Albans 83, 84, 85, 86
Stanborough Park 90
Standon 56
Standon Green End 57
Stevenage 23, 24
Stratton's Folly 103

Therfield 49
Therfield Heath 44, 47, 48
Tring 72

Verulamium 87, 88, 89

Waltham Cross 106
Watford 109, 123, 124, 125
Watton-at-Stone 55
Welwyn Garden City 9, 27
Westmill 58
Wheathampstead 26
Willian 28
Wilstone 69
Woolmers 102